29.90

Heinemann
First
Encyclopedia

Volume 6

Lib-Net

Heinemann Library
Chicago, Illinois

© 1999 Reed Educational & Professional Publishing
Published by Heinemann Library,
an imprint of Reed Educational & Professional Publishing,
Chicago, IL 60602
Customer Service: 888-454-2279
Visit our website at www.heinemannlibrary.com

Series Editors: Rebecca and Stephen Vickers
Author Team: Rob Alcraft, Catherine Chambers, Jim Drake,
Fred Martin, Angela Royston, Jane Shuter, Roger Thomas,
Rebecca Vickers, Stephen Vickers

Photo research by Katharine Smith
Designed and Typeset by Gecko Ltd
Printed in Hong Kong, China

03 02 01 00
10 9 8 7 6 5 4 3 2

Library of Congress Cataloging-in-Publication Data

Heinemann first encyclopedia.
     p.   cm.
    Summary: A ten-volume encyclopedia covering animals, plants,
countries, transportation, science, ancient civilizations, and world
history.
    ISBN 1-57572-741-2 (lib. bdg.)
    1. Children's encyclopedias and dictionaries. [1. Encyclopedias
and dictionaries.] I. Heinemann Library (Firm)
AG5.H45   1998
031—dc21   98-20016
                                      CIP
                                      AC

Acknowledgments

Cover: The cover illustration is of a male specimen of Ornithoptera goliath, commonly called the Goliath Birdwing. Special thanks to Dr. George C.
McGavin and the Hope Entomological Collections, Oxford University Museum of Natural History; J. Allan Cash Ltd., pp. 4, 14, 7, 27, 47, 48;
Bridgeman Art Library, pp. 8 top, 28; John Cleare Mountain Camera, p. 19; Trevor Clifford Photography, p. 21 bottom; Chris Honeywell, p. 24 top;
Bruce Coleman/Alain Compost, p. 18 bottom; Jeff Foot, p. 31 bottom; Corbis-Bettman, p. 45; Michael Holford/British Museum, p. 10 bottom;
Hulton Getty, p. 40 bottom; The Hutchison Library/Bernard Regent, p. 36; Oxford Scientific Film, p. 5 bottom; Waina Cheng, p. 11 top; J.A.L.
Cooke, p. 37 bottom; Kenneth Day, p. 20 bottom; Michael Fogden, p. 22; David C. Fritts, p. 33 bottom; Mike Hill, p. 33 top; Michael Leach, p. 42
bottom; Zig Leszczynski, p. 30 bottom; Renee Lynn, p. 9 top; Fred McConnaughey, p. 31 top; John Mitchell, p. 39 top; Lloyd Nielsen, p. 20 top; Stan
Osolinski, p. 35; Peter Parks, p. 5 top; Keith Ringland, p. 29; Norbert Rosing, p. 9 bottom; Frithjof Skibbe, p. 38; Michael R. Stoklos, p. 8 bottom;
Survival Anglia/Doug Allan, p. 15; Survival Anglia/Danial Vall, p. 41; K.G. Vock, p. 39 bottom; Barrie E. Watts, pp. 18 top, 42 top; W. Wisniewski,
p. 11 bottom; Redferns, pp. 4, 43; Science Photo Library/David Guyon, p. 24 bottom; Pekka Parvianen, p. 26 bottom; John Sandford, p. 26 top;
Stock Market, p. 7 bottom; Tony Stone Worldwide/Byron Jorjorian, p. 7 top; Reg Watson, p. 23; Zefa, p. 40 top.

Welcome to
Heinemann First Encyclopedia

What is an encyclopedia?

An encyclopedia is an information book. It gives the most important facts about many different subjects. This encyclopedia has been written for children who are using an encyclopedia for the first time. It covers many of the subjects from school and others you may find interesting.

What is in this encyclopedia?

In this encyclopedia, each topic is called an *entry*. There is one page of information for every entry. The entries in this encyclopedia explain

- animals
- plants
- dinosaurs
- countries
- geography
- history
- world religions
- music
- art
- transportation
- science
- technology

How to use this encyclopedia

This encyclopedia has eleven books called *volumes*. The first ten volumes contain entries. The entries are all in alphabetical order. This means that Volume 1 starts with entries that begin with the letter *A* and Volume 10 ends with entries that begin with the letter *Z*. Volume 11 is the index volume. It also has interesting information about American history.

Here are two entries that show you what you can find on a page:

The "see also" line tells you where to find other related information.

This is the letter that the entry starts with.

Fact boxes give you details about the topic.

Did You Know? boxes have fun or interesting bits of information.

The Fact File tells you important facts and figures.

Libya

see also: Africa, Desert

Libya is a country in northern Africa. Libya is almost all desert. The land is mostly flat. It has a few low mountains. The coast is cooler and sometimes has rain.

Living in Libya

Most Libyans live in cities on the coast. Oil and natural gas were discovered in Libya in 1959. This made Libya a rich country.

Farmers in the north grow dates, olives, citrus fruits, grapes, and wheat. Sheep, goats, cattle, and camels graze where there is enough grass for them to eat.

There are no rivers that flow all year round. The people need more water for farming, drinking, and washing. Libya is working to bring water from one end of the country to the other.

These Tuareg men in southern Libya are performing a traditional dance.

DID YOU KNOW?

The highest temperature ever recorded was in Libya in 1922. It was 136°F.

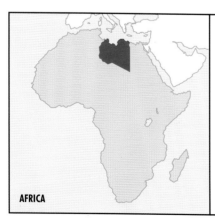

AFRICA

FACT FILE

PEOPLE	Libyans
POPULATION	about 5 million
MAIN LANGUAGES	Arabic, Berber, Italian, English
CAPITAL CITY	Tripoli
MONEY	Libyan dinar
HIGHEST MOUNTAIN	Bette Peak—7,503 feet
LONGEST RIVER	Rivers flow only when it rains.

Lice

see also: Insects

Lice are small insects. They have no wings. They have very fat bodies. Lice live in the clothes, hair, feathers, and fur of people and animals.

Lice families

An adult female louse lays tiny eggs. The eggs are called nits. The nits take a week or two to hatch. Lice move from person to person. Head lice spread quickly wherever there are lots of people. Lice spread quickly in camps and schools. They can make the skin and head itch.

LICE FACTS

NUMBER OF KINDS	3,300
COLOR	brown or yellow-brown
SIZE	much less than one inch
STATUS	common
LIFE SPAN	one month
ENEMIES	special chemicals called insecticides

tube for sucking up blood

body swells up with blood

claws for gripping hair and fur

a human head louse

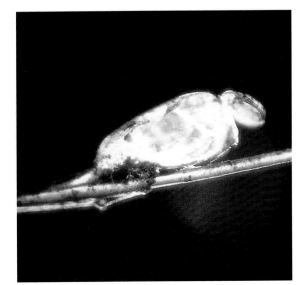

A head louse egg sticks to hair.

MEAT EATER

Lice poke a hole in the skin of their victims. Then they suck up blood. There are different types of lice. Some types of lice live on humans. Some lice live on other mammals. Some lice live on birds.

Life Cycle

see also: Flower, Metamorphosis

A life cycle is all the stages in the life of an animal or plant. A life cycle includes the start of life, the process of growing, having young, and then dying. Different living things have different stages in their life cycles.

Plant life cycle

A flowering plant starts its life cycle as a seed. The baby plant grows in the seed. The baby plant grows leaves and roots. It gets bigger. The new plant flowers. Its male pollen transfers to the female part of the flower. Then a new fruit with a seed grows.

DID YOU KNOW?

- Most insects have four stages to their life cycle: egg, larva, pupa, adult.
- Some insects, like grasshoppers, have only three stages: egg, nymph, adult.
- Amphibians have three stages: egg, tadpole, adult.
- Reptiles and birds lay eggs that hatch. The young grow into adults.

Human life cycle

Humans have a life cycle. It is like the life cycle of most other mammals. A human starts as an egg in a female's body. The fertilized egg grows into a baby inside the mother. This takes about 40 weeks. The parents care for the baby after he or she is born. The newborn baby is fed on milk. The baby grows. It begins to eat regular food.

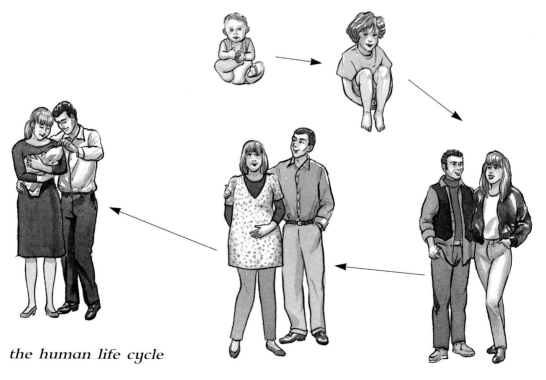

the human life cycle

Light

see also: Color, Energy, Sun

Light is a form of energy. Light helps us to see. We can only see things when light bounces off them and into our eyes.

DID YOU KNOW?

Shadows are caused when light cannot pass through an object. The light is on one side of the object. The shadow is on the other side.

The sun and light

Light on Earth comes from the sun. All food eaten on Earth needed light from the sun at some point. Other kinds of fuel also needed sunlight at some time. Wood and gas formed from plants that grew in sunlight. Electricity is made using fuel that comes from plants that grew in sunlight.

Big cities are lit up with bright lights at night.

How light works

Light always travels in straight lines. Nothing travels faster than light. The sun is 93 million miles from Earth. It only takes eight minutes for the light from the sun to travel to Earth. Light bounces off shiny surfaces. It bounces off mirrors and polished metal. This is called reflection. Rays of light bend when they pass through water or clear glass. This is called refraction.

The sun is the source of all Earth's light energy.

Lightning

see also: Electricity, Weather

Lightning is a giant electric spark. It makes a bright flash of light in the sky. Thunder is the noise that follows the lightning. Thunder is heard because lightning heats the air as it moves through it. Light moves faster than sound. That is why we see the lightning flash and then we hear the thunder.

What causes lightning?

Lightning happens when energy in clouds turns into electrical energy. Lightning strikes when the electrical energy jumps to the ground or to another cloud. Lightning sometimes strikes buildings and tall trees. Tall buildings are usually safe from lightning. The tops of tall buildings have lightning conductors. This sends the electric energy down a thick wire into the ground.

Benjamin Franklin (1706–1790)

Benjamin Franklin was an American scientist and politician. He flew a kite in a thunderstorm to show that lightning was electricity. The lightning struck the kite. It came down the wet string. This was very dangerous. He was lucky not to have been killed.

STAY SAFE!

If you are caught in a thunderstorm:
- Don't stay in the open or on hills.
- Find shelter inside a building or a car, *not* under trees.
- If you are swimming or boating, get out of the water and find shelter.
- Don't talk on the telephone unless it is a cellular phone with no wires.

Cloud-to-ground lightning is the most familiar.

Lion

see also: Africa, Cat, Mammals

A lion is a mammal. It is a large member of the cat family. Most lions live on the hot, grassy plains of Africa. A few lions live in India. Lions are strong, fast hunters. They sleep or rest about 20 hours a day.

LION FACTS

COLOR	light brown
LENGTH	up to 9 feet
WEIGHT	up to 400 lbs.
STATUS	common
LIFE SPAN	about 20 years
ENEMIES	cheetahs, hyenas, people

Lion families

A male is called a lion. A female is called a lioness. Baby lions are called cubs. A lioness will have two or three cubs at a time. Lions, lionesses, and their cubs live together in a group called a *pride*. The pride lives and hunts in one place. This place is called their territory.

sharp teeth for eating meat

hairy mane on male lions to look fierce and to protect them when fighting

strong legs for running in short, fast bursts

sharp claws for hunting

a lion

A lioness always watches for enemies that might attack her cubs.

MEAT EATER

A lion can eat 88 pounds of meat at one meal. The lion then spends several days sleeping off the meal. Lions usually hunt for animals such as zebra, wildebeest, and antelope.

Literature

see also: Drama, Poetry, Story

Literature is writing that is meant for other people to read. Literature may be stories, plays, poetry, or information. Some languages have no written form. They have no literature.

Literature is recorded in books, tapes, videos, and CDs.

The first literature

People have always used literature for two main reasons. First, they wrote down what had happened. They recorded their history. Second, people used writing to record stories, poems, and messages for entertainment.

Literature today

Literature grew into many forms as more people learned to read and write. Many writers wrote books. The books are filled with stories, drama, and poetry. People also watch plays in theaters. They listen to cassette tapes of stories and plays. Many TV programs and videos are works of literature. Today new literature can also be found on the internet.

DID YOU KNOW?

The earliest form of writing that did not use pictures was called cuneiform. It was invented in Sumer in the Middle East about 4,000 years ago.

Cuneiform writing was made on clay tablets. This was the first literature.

Lizard

see also: Reptiles

The lizard is a reptile. There are many kinds of lizards all over the world. Most lizards are small. A few, like monitor lizards, are large. The Komodo dragon is ten feet long. Some lizards climb trees. Other lizards live on the ground.

LIZARD FACTS

NUMBER OF KINDS	3,700
COLOR	usually greenish-brown
LENGTH	5 inches to 10 feet
WEIGHT	2 oz. to 132 lbs.
STATUS	some are rare or threatened
LIFE SPAN	6 to 50 years
ENEMIES	snakes, birds, larger lizards

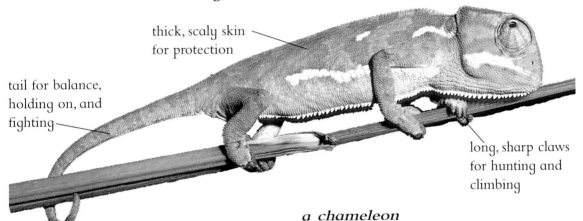

thick, scaly skin for protection

tail for balance, holding on, and fighting

long, sharp claws for hunting and climbing

a chameleon

This marine iguana baby rides on its mother's back when she climbs.

Lizard families

Some female lizards lay their eggs in soil. The soil needs to be warm to keep the eggs at the right temperature. The babies hatch after a few weeks. Other lizards keep the eggs inside them until the eggs are ready to hatch.

PLANT, INSECT, AND MEAT EATER

Lizards use their tongues to taste the air as they look for food. Most lizards eat insects and plants. Large lizards eat mammals.

Lung

see also: Air, Human Body, Oxygen

Lungs are organs. People and animals use lungs for breathing. Lungs breathe in oxygen from the air. Lungs breathe out carbon dioxide.

Breathing

Breathing in air is called *inhaling*. Breathing out is called *exhaling*. Air is inhaled through the nose and mouth. The muscles in the chest push the air in and out of the lungs. Special hairs in the nose catch dust so it doesn't get to the lungs. The air goes down the windpipe into the lungs. The air goes through smaller and smaller tubes in the lungs.

At the end of the small tubes are many tiny air sacs called *alveoli.* Blood goes to the alveoli. Blood collects oxygen from the lungs. Blood gets rid of carbon dioxide.

Lung problems

Dirt and pollution can harm the lungs. Coughing is caused by the lungs squeezing together to get rid of the dirt inside.

DID YOU KNOW?

If the alveoli from both lungs of an adult were flattened out, they would cover a space the size of a tennis court.

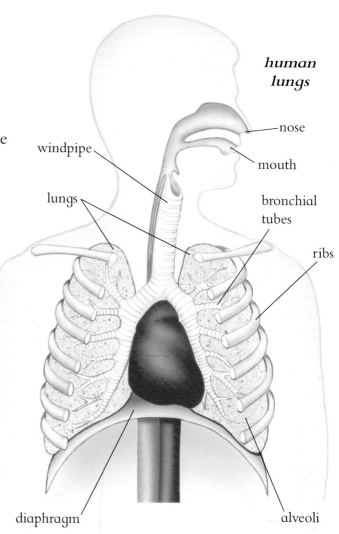

human lungs

nose

mouth

windpipe

bronchial tubes

lungs

ribs

diaphragm

alveoli

STAY HEALTHY!

Keep your lungs healthy by never smoking cigarettes. Wear a mask when you do a dusty job. Try not to walk along main roads where you will breathe in exhaust fumes from cars, buses, and trucks.

Luxembourg

see also: Europe

Luxembourg is one of the smallest countries in Europe. It is mostly hills and high, flat land. One-third of the country has forests. The rest of the land is used for growing grass or crops. The summer is warm. The winter can be cold and snowy.

Living in Luxembourg

Almost all of the people work in the towns and cities. Factories make steel, glass, car tires, and chemicals. Most people work in banks and other office jobs.

Luxembourg has a royal family. It is headed by the Grand Duke. Tourists come to Luxembourg to visit old castles and to see the landscape.

This is the flower market in Luxembourg.

DID YOU KNOW?

Luxembourg has 100 percent literacy. That means everyone can read and write.

EUROPE

FACT FILE

PEOPLE.................... Luxembourgers

POPULATION............425 thousand

MAIN LANGUAGES....Letzeburgesch, French, German

CAPITAL CITY..........Luxembourg

MONEY................... Euro

HIGHEST MOUNTAIN..............Buurgplaatz–1,835 feet

LONGEST RIVER.......River Moselle–320 miles

Machines, Simple

see also: Energy

A machine helps people to do work quickly or easily. A machine can push or pull. A machine can turn a small movement into a big movement, or turn a big movement into a small movement. Six simple machines are what make all big machines work.

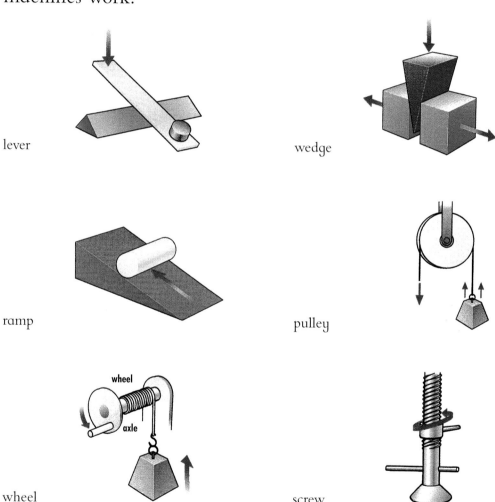

lever

wedge

ramp

pulley

wheel

screw

These are six different types of simple machines.

DID YOU KNOW?

Playground equipment such as slides, swings, and see-saws are simple machines.

Madagascar

see also: Africa, Island

Madagascar is an island country. It is off the east coast of Africa. It is the world's fourth biggest island. There are mountains in the middle of Madagascar. Most of the low land and rivers are in the west. There are some rainforests. There are coral reefs along the east coast. The weather is mostly hot and wet.

Living in Madagascar

About three fourths of the people live in the rural areas. They work on farms. Farmers grow rice, vegetables, and fruit. People who live on the coast go fishing. People grow or catch the food they eat. Rice and vegetables are their main foods. Most food is cooked with hot spices, peppers, and strong sauces. Coffee, cloves, and vanilla are also grown. They are sold to other countries.

This is the fruit and vegetable market in the city of Mahajanga.

DID YOU KNOW?

Madagascar is important as a home for wildlife. There are 150 thousand animals on the island that are not found anywhere else in the world. One of these animals is the lemur. It is related to the monkey.

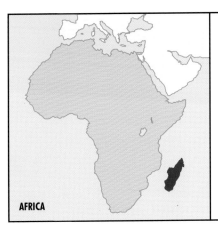

AFRICA

FACT FILE

PEOPLE	Malagasy
POPULATION	about 14 million
MAIN LANGUAGES	Malagasy, French
CAPITAL CITY	Antananarivo
MONEY	Malagasy franc
HIGHEST MOUNTAIN	Mount Maromokotro–9,439 feet
LONGEST RIVER	River Mangoky–348 miles

Magnet

see also: Metal

A magnet is a piece of metal. It is usually made of iron or steel. A magnet pulls another metal towards it. Every magnet has two ends. They are called poles. One pole of a magnet is pulled towards Earth's North Pole. This is called the magnet's north pole. The other end of the magnet is called the magnet's south pole.

How magnets work

If the ends or poles of two magnets are brought close to each other and they are the same poles, the magnets will push each other away. This is called *repulsion.* If the two poles are different, then the magnets will pull toward each other. This is called *attraction.*

DID YOU KNOW?

A magnet can be used to tell if a can is made from steel or aluminium. Steel cans will stick to a magnet. Aluminum cans will not stick.

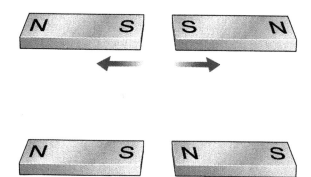

The arrows show that like poles repel and opposite poles attract.

How magnets are used

- A compass has a magnetic needle. It spins to point to Earth's North Pole
- Magnets can be used as door catches.
- Recording tapes and computer disks are magnetic. There are millions of tiny magnets mixed into the plastic.
- Radios, televisions, and stereo systems have magnets in the speakers where the sound comes out.
- Hospitals use magnets in a machine that takes pictures of the inside of human bodies. This is called MRI.

One end of a horseshoe-shaped magnet is the south pole. The other end is the north pole.

Malaysia

see also: Asia, Rainforest

Malaysia is a country with two parts. One part of the country is on the southeast tip of Asia. The other part is on the northern part of the island of Borneo. Both parts of Malaysia are mostly mountains and forests. The climate is hot and wet.

These women are drying cuttlefish to sell as food.

Living in Malaysia

Half of the people live in the rural areas. The farms grow rice, cocoa, and oil palms. People living by the coasts catch fish. There are many trees in the Malaysian rainforest. Some are cut down for wood. Other trees are tapped for their rubber sap. Malaysia also has factories which make cars, electronic products, and other things.

The people of Malaysia are Malays, Chinese, and people from India. Malaysia's food, houses, and clothing come from these three cultures. The most well-known Malay food is *satay*. This is grilled meat on a stick. It is usually served with spicy peanut sauce.

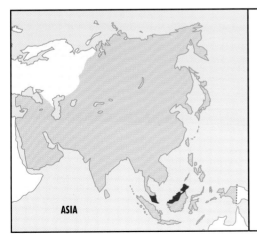

ASIA

FACT FILE

PEOPLE........................ Malaysian

POPULATION .... about 22 million

MAIN LANGUAGES....... Bahasa Malaysia, English, Chinese

CAPITAL CITY............. Kuala Lumpur

MONEY....................... Ringgit

HIGHEST MOUNTAIN... Kinabalu—13,459 feet

LONGEST RIVER.......... River Rajang—350 miles

Mammal

see also: Animals, Vertebrate

Mammal is the name given to a group of animals. There are more than 4,000 different kinds of mammals.

The smallest mammal is the shrew. It weighs less than one tenth of an ounce.

What makes a mammal?
All mammals have hair or fur. Most mammal babies are born alive out of the mother. Mammals feed on their mother's milk when they are born. Mammals make heat using energy from the food they eat. They are warm-blooded animals.

Only two mammals lay eggs. They are the spiny anteaters, like the one shown here, and the platypus.

Where do mammals live?
Mammals have lived on Earth since the time of the dinosaurs. Mammals live everywhere. They live on the ground, in the trees, and in the water. Some mammals, called bats, can even fly. Each mammal's body is different. Its body fits its way of life. For example, polar bears have thick, warm coats of white fur. They live in the freezing, snowy Arctic.

DID YOU KNOW?

The largest living mammal is the blue whale. It weighs more than 110 tons and is 102 feet long.

Map

A map is a drawing of land as it would look from above. A map that shows the details of a very small area is called a plan. Maps of the seas and oceans are called charts.

Using maps

Some maps only show roads. They help people travel from one place to another. Some maps are weather maps or maps of the stars in the sky. Maps can be bound in a book called an *atlas.* Maps can also be put on large sheets of paper. The paper can be folded and carried around. A globe is a round map of the earth.

People use maps to find their way around unfamiliar places.

What is on a map?

All maps have three special things. They have a compass point. The compass point shows the north, south, east, and west directions on the map. They have a distance scale. The scale shows how far it is from one place to another on the map. They have a key or legend. The key or legend gives the meanings of all the symbols on the map.

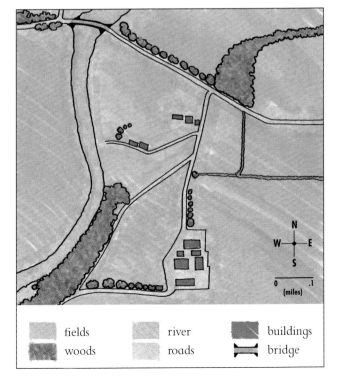

This simple map shows a river, roads, and some buildings.

Marsupial

see also: Australia, Kangaroo, Koala, Mammal, Opossum

Marsupials are mammals. A female marsupial has a pocket called a pouch. The babies live in the pouch. Kangaroos and koalas are marsupials. Marsupials are found in Australia, Papua New Guinea, North America, and South America.

Marsupial babies

All marsupial babies are born very small, hairless, and blind. A newborn marsupial baby crawls through the mother's fur. It crawls into her pouch. The baby stays in the pouch. It drinks milk. It grows until it is big enough to live outside of the pouch.

Baby kangaroos are called joeys. They are less than one inch long when they are born. When the joey gets bigger, it hops in and out of its mother's pouch. Opossum babies ride on their mother's back when they get too big to be in the pouch.

MARSUPIAL FACTS

NUMBER OF KINDS	250
LARGEST	red kangaroo can weigh up to 198 lbs.
SMALLEST	pilbra ningaui—much less than one ounce
FASTEST	kangaroos can bound along at 37 mph

The brush-tailed possum is a marsupial from Australia. It is related to the American opossum.

The kangaroo joey lives in its mother's pouch. This joey will soon be too big to get in and out of the pouch.

Matter

see also: Temperature

Matter makes up everything around us. All matter on Earth is in one of three forms. These forms are solid, liquid, and gas.

Solids, liquids, and gases

- Solids keep their shape and size. Solids cannot be squashed into a smaller space or stretched into a bigger space.
- All liquids can be poured. Liquids change their shape to fit the container into which they are poured.
- Gases can change their shape. They spread out to fill the space they are in.

Most matter can be in any of the three forms at different times. For example, frozen water is ice. That is a solid. Water at temperatures between 32°F and 212°F is a liquid. Water that is heated to more than 212°F turns into steam. Steam is a gas.

DID YOU KNOW?

All matter is made of very small particles. The particles are too small to see. These particles are called *atoms*. Most matter is made up of different atoms.

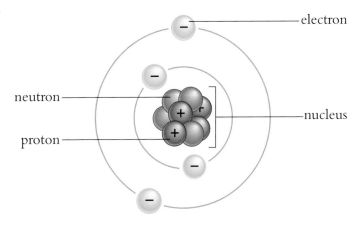

the parts of an atom

Here is water in its three forms—steamy gas, liquid water, and solid ice.

Maya

see also: Aztecs, Hieroglyphic, Incas, Pyramid

The Maya were a Native American people. They lived about 1,500 years ago. The Maya ruled parts of what is now Central America. The Maya took over many small groups of people. They formed one big country. This was called the Mayan Empire. The Maya were powerful between A.D.300 and A.D.900.

DID YOU KNOW?

Mayan priests invented a 365 day calendar. It was more accurate than calendars used in the rest of the world.

What were the Maya like?

The Maya were organized into small groups. Each group had its own king. One person might have ruled all the groups. There were also priests, warriors, traders, and farmers. Farmers grew crops in the fields. The Maya believed in many gods and goddesses.

KEY DATES

1500 B.C.	first Mayan groups settle in what is now Mexico
A.D.300–900	Mayan Empire grows; cities are built; the Mayan people trade
A.D.900	Mayan groups break up
A.D.1520	Spanish move into the area

Mayan step pyramids, like this one, were used to worship the gods and goddesses.

What are the Maya known for?

The Maya built stone, step pyramids. They made beautiful pottery. They used picture writing called hieroglyphics.

What happened to the Maya?

The Mayan Empire began to fall apart in about A.D.900. No one knows why this happened. They may have been invaded by other tribes. Some Maya moved south. They were taken over by the Spanish. There are still Mayan people in most of the countries in Central America.

Measurement

see also: Calendar, Numbers, Time

Measurement tells the size of an object or the number of things in a group. Measurement is also a way to find the right size or the right number. Measurement makes sure that things like cakes and medicines are the same every time.

The first measurements

The first measurements were units that could be found anywhere. Parts of the human body were used for measuring in ancient Egypt. For example, a cubit was the length of an arm from the tip of the middle finger to the elbow. Not everyone is the same size, so these measurements were not always the same.

The metric system

About 200 years ago the metric system was first used in France. Now the metric system is used around the world.

DIFFERENT METRIC UNITS

Length: kilometers (km), meters (m), centimeters (cm), millimeters (mm)
   10 mm = 1 cm
   100 cm = 1 m
   1000 m = 1 km

Mass: metric tons (t), kilograms (kg), grams (g), milligrams (mg)
   1000 mg = 1 g
   1000 g = 1 kg
   1000 kg = 1 t

Capacity: liters (l), milliliters (ml)
   1000 ml = 1 l

Time: seconds, minutes, hours, days, months
   60 seconds = 1 minute
   60 minutes = 1 hour
   24 hours = 1 day
   28–31 days = 1 month
   12 months = 1 year

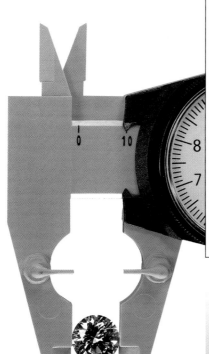

This diamond is being measured. The gauge tells how wide it is.

DID YOU KNOW?

Some old units are still used for special things. The weight of diamonds are measured in carats. A carat is based on the weight of a carob bean.

Metal

see also: Rock, Magnet, Meteor

Metals are solid materials. Metals can be made into shapes. Some metals are strong, shiny, and hard. Other metals are weak, dull, and soft. Most metals are found in rocks in the ground. Rocks containing metal are called *ores*.

Properties of metals

Electricity and heat pass through metal. This is called *conduction*. Most electric wires are made of the metal called copper. Copper conducts electricity. Copper can be bent and stretched into wires.

Metals can be mixed together. Mixed metals are called *alloys*. An alloy can be better than each metal by itself. Bronze is an alloy made of copper and tin. Bronze is stronger than copper or tin.

DID YOU KNOW?

Potassium is a soft metal. It is about as hard as cheese. Potassium bursts into flames when it touches water.

Gold is a valuable metal. It has been used for thousands of years. This gold mask covered of the mummy of Egyptian pharoah Tutankhamen.

Using metals today

Important metals are iron alloys, copper, and aluminum. Many alloys containing iron are called steel. Steel is very strong and heavy. It is used to make skyscrapers, ships, and cars. Aluminum is strong and light. It is used to make pots and pans and drink cans.

Steel is heated until it is red-hot. Then the steel is rolled into shape.

Metamorphosis

see also: Amphibians, Insects, Life Cycle

The word *metamorphosis* means "change." Metamorphosis is what happens to some insects as they go through different stages in their lives.

The metamorphosis of a butterfly

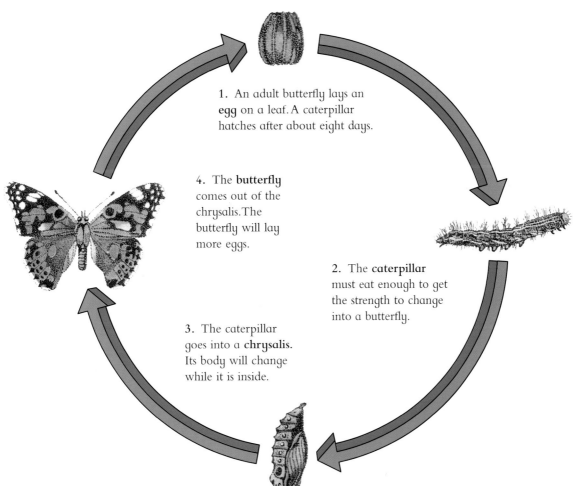

1. An adult butterfly lays an **egg** on a leaf. A caterpillar hatches after about eight days.

2. The **caterpillar** must eat enough to get the strength to change into a butterfly.

3. The caterpillar goes into a **chrysalis**. Its body will change while it is inside.

4. The **butterfly** comes out of the chrysalis. The butterfly will lay more eggs.

Fast and slow changes

All insects and some amphibians go through a metamorphosis. This change is complete and sudden for insects like butterflies. For other insects, such as grasshoppers, the change is slower.

A grasshopper changes its skin four or five times as it grows. It becomes more like an adult grasshopper each time it changes. The new skin is soft and wet. The new skin gets harder as it dries.

Meteor

see also: Earth, Solar System

A meteor is a piece of rock or metal. It flies through space. Meteors that enter the earth's atmosphere are sometimes called *shooting* or *falling stars*.

Watching for meteors

The earth meets millions of meteors every day as it moves through space. These meteors can sometimes be seen in the sky on a clear, dark night. A bright meteor may leave a glowing trail behind it. Some meteors are in groups. The group might be seen as a meteor shower. These showers often come from the tails of comets.

As a meteor enters the earth's atmosphere, it burns up. This causes the bright streak of light in the sky.

DID YOU KNOW?

Some meteor showers last a few days. They can be seen at the same time and in the same place in the sky every year.

This meteorite crater in Arizona is nearly a mile across. It was made about 25 thousand years ago.

Meteorites

Meteorites are meteors that reach the earth. They did not burn up in the earth's atmosphere. Meteorites may be pieces of other planets. They may come from other solar systems. Most meteorites are the size of dust. Sometimes a big meteorite will hit the ground very hard. The hole it makes is called a *crater.* Many giant meteorites hit the earth billions of years ago. Most of the craters that they made were worn down by wind and rain. Some of these craters filled with water. The moon has been hit by meteorites. The moon's craters can be seen from earth.

Mexico

see also: Aztecs, Maya, North America

Mexico is a country in North America. There are mountains in the west and near the Gulf of Mexico. There is high, flat land between the mountains. This land is warm and dry. The coastal lowlands are hot and wet.

DID YOU KNOW?

Mexico City is built on top of the Aztec city called Tenochtitlan. This was a city on an island in a lake.

Living in Mexico

Many Mexicans live in the cities. They work in businesses, factories, and with tourists. Farmers grow corn, beans, and vegetables for their families. Big farms grow cotton, coffee, and fruit to sell in Mexico and in other countries.

Almost anything can be bought in Mexico's open markets. This stall sells fruits and vegetables.

Mexicans are a mix of Native Americans and people who came from Spain. Some of the foods, like enchiladas, come from the Indian cultures.

NORTH AMERICA

FACT FILE

PEOPLE . . . . Mexicans
POPULATION . . . . about 100 million
MAIN LANGUAGE . . . . Spanish
CAPITAL CITY . . . . Mexico City
MONEY . . . . Peso
HIGHEST
MOUNTAIN . . . . Pico de Orizaba—18,707 feet
LONGEST RIVER . . . . . Rio Bravo Del Norte—1,885 miles

Middle Ages

see also: Castle, Cathedral, Knight

The Middle Ages is a time in the history of Europe. It is the time between the fall of the Roman Empire and the Renaissance.

What happened in the Middle Ages?

At the beginning of the Middle Ages, small areas of Europe each had their own rulers. Then most of Europe became Christian. Europe was united by religion. People began to build towns and cities. They traded with each other. There was less fighting. Europe became richer. Europeans built cathedrals, castles, and universities. At the beginning of the Middle Ages, only people who were part of the church could read and write. By the end of the Middle Ages, many more people could read and write.

What happened next?

The Middle Ages did not suddenly stop. One by one, countries moved into the time called the Renaissance.

By the end of the Middle Ages, more people lived in towns and cities. These people are making hay outside the city walls.

KEY DATES

A.D. 476 ..... fall of the Roman Empire

A.D. 800 ..... most of Europe unites under Emperor Charlemagne

A.D. 1066 ... William of Normandy conquers England

A.D. 1100 ..... universities begin

A.D. 1130 ..... first school for doctors opens

A.D. 1330 ..... Renaissance begins in Italy

A.D. 1450 ..... Renaissance spreads through Europe

Migration

see also: Animals

Migration is a kind of journey made by an animal. It can be a journey to find a mate. It can be a journey to find food. It can be a journey to find the right kind of weather. Different kinds of animals migrate. Sometimes people migrate.

DID YOU KNOW?

No one really knows how animals know where to migrate. Birds seem to have a built-in compass. They are able to find their way even in the dark. Salmon may smell the rivers where they were born.

Why migrate?

Most migrating animals leave an area when winter comes. They travel to warmer places. They may have longer days and plenty of food in the warmer place. The animals leave the winter area when spring comes. They return to their summer home.

Young salmon are born in rivers. Then they swim out to sea. They stay in the sea for a year or two. The salmon return to the river where they were born. They swim up the river against the current. They migrate to where they were born.

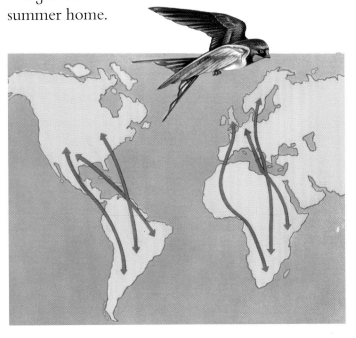

Migrating swallows leave their homes in the fall. These birds spend the winter in Africa or South America. They fly back home in the spring. Each way of their journey can be as much as 6,200 miles.

Mining

see also: Metal, Rock

Mining means digging things out of the earth. Most mining takes rocks, minerals, metals, oil, gas, and coal from the earth.

Types of mining

Rocks near the surface of the ground can be dug from a pit. This is called *strip mining*. Giant mechanical shovels scoop up the rocks. Other things are mined from deep under the ground. A mine shaft is dug down until it reaches the layer to be mined. Then explosives, drills, and giant cutters are used to do the mining. Oil and gas are mined by drilling holes deep into the ground. Then the oil or gas comes up to the surface on its own, or it is pumped up.

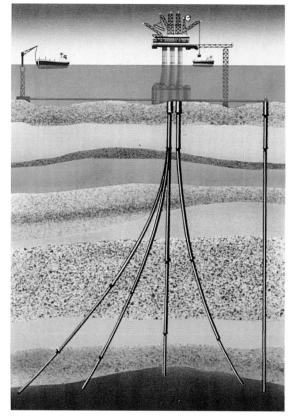

Oil and gas are pumped up from deep under the sea floor.

Copper is mined from this strip mine in Arizona.

People and mining

People have dug mines for thousands of years. Mining gets people what they want from the earth. Salt is mined to use in cooking and preserving food. Coal, gas, and oil are mined to use as fuel to make electricity and heat. They are also fuel for transportation.

DID YOU KNOW?

Some precious metals and rocks are used to make jewelry. Silver, gold, diamonds, and rubies all come from mines.

Mollusk

see also: Animals, Invertebrate

Mollusks are invertebrates. They are animals with soft bodies. There are more than 70 thousand kinds of mollusks. Some mollusks have shells. The shells of cuttlefish and squid are inside their bodies.

Mollusk families

All mollusks lay eggs. Most female mollusks lay eggs on plants or in the water. The eggs hatch on their own. The babies find food for themselves.

Some mollusks look after their eggs. The female giant octopus protects her eggs for six months. She never leaves her nest, not even to find food for herself.

This large clam lives on the bottom of the sea.

Where mollusks live

Some mollusks, such as some snails and slugs, live on land. They crawl over leaves and eat the leaves. Squid and octopuses live in saltwater seas. They eat fish and other water creatures. Shellfish live on rocks under the sea. They eat tiny animals and plants called plankton from the seawater. There are freshwater clams and oysters living in rivers and lakes. They eat tiny freshwater creatures.

There are eight plates in the shell of this mollusk. It is called a chiton.

DID YOU KNOW?

The largest mollusk in the world is the giant squid. It can grow as long as 50 feet. That is longer than a bus.

Money

Money is used by people to buy things they need. People are given money in exchange for things they sell or for work they do.

Why use money?

People did not use money hundreds of years ago. They swapped things with each other. This is called bartering. Later, people used shells, cocoa beans, or bits of metal to swap for the things they needed. This was easier than bartering.

Real money

The first real money was metal coins. Then governments began to make paper money. Every country makes its own money. The coins and paper money look different. They have different names.

Plastic money

A credit card or charge card is a plastic card. It has a name and an account number on it. The card can be used to pay for things. The credit card company pays the business. Then the credit card company collects the money from the person whose name is on the card. Some people call credit cards "plastic money."

Here is money from Uganda, Brazil, the United States, the United Kingdom, and Australia.

DID YOU KNOW?

Checks are a kind of money. Checks can be filled in with whatever amount of money is needed. The person who writes the check has to have that amount of money in the bank.

Monkey

see also: Ape, Mammals

A monkey is a mammal. It belongs to the same group of mammals as apes and human beings. They live in Africa, Asia, and South America. Monkeys have strong arms and legs. They are good climbers and runners.

Monkey families

Monkeys live in groups called *troops*. The strongest male monkey is the leader. Each troop has several female monkeys and their babies. A female monkey usuallyhas one baby at a time.

strong tail to use as an extra arm for climbing and for balance

MONKEY FACTS

NUMBER OF	
KINDS	about 400
COLOR.........	usually brown, black, white, or gray
HEIGHT	5 inches to 3 feet
WEIGHT	2 oz. to 100 lbs.
STATUS........	some types are endangered
LIFE SPAN......	up to 18 years
ENEMIES	birds, snakes, larger animals, people

fur for keeping warm

hands have fingers and feet have toes for holding and picking up things

a baboon

This baby squirrel monkey is with its mother and a brother or sister.

PLANT, INSECT, AND MEAT EATER

Monkeys move from place to place. They eat fruit and leaves. Monkeys peel fruit with their fingers and teeth. Some monkeys also eat insects and small mammals.

Moon

see also: Earth, Solar System, Space Exploration, Sun

The moon is a big ball of rock. It travels around the earth. Its path is called an *orbit*. It is the brightest thing in the night sky.

The moon's phases

Every month the moon goes through phases. First it looks like a thin crescent. Then it seems to grow to a full circle. Finally, it shrinks back again. The moon takes about 29½ days for each orbit around the earth.

The same side of the moon always faces the earth. The moon does not give out light. It is lit by the sun's light reflecting off the moon's surface.

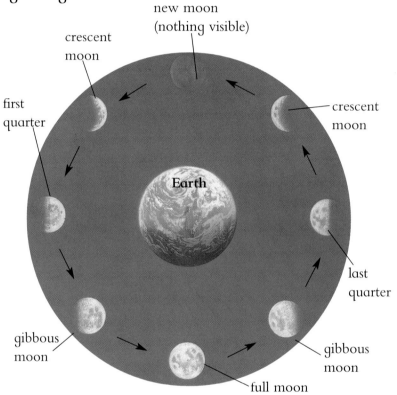

The moon only seems to change shape. This is because the light shining on it from the sun is blocked by the earth. This picture shows the phases of the moon as it orbits the earth.

On the moon

The patterns that can be seen on the moon are its mountains, craters, and plains. Most of the moon's craters are billions of years old. There is no air or water on the moon to wear away the mountains and craters. In July 1969, the U.S. space mission Apollo 11 flew to the moon. The commander, Neil Armstrong, was the first person to walk on the moon.

DID YOU KNOW?

Other planets in our solar system also have orbiting moons. Saturn has the most moons. It has at least 18.

Moose

see also: Arctic, Deer

The moose is a mammal. It is the largest deer in the world. Moose live in forests in the northern parts of the world. Moose walk into lakes during the summer. They eat the water plants and cool off in the water.

Moose families

The male moose is called a bull. The female moose is called a cow. Male moose live on their own. They fight over the females every autumn. The female moose has one or two babies in the spring. These babies are called calves. Calves may stay with their mother for a year.

MOOSE FACTS

NUMBER OF KINDS	6
COLOR	brown with lighter brown legs
LENGTH	up to 10 feet
HEIGHT	up to 8 feet
WEIGHT	880 to 1,800 lbs.
STATUS	common
LIFE SPAN	about 20 years
ENEMIES	wolves, cougars, people

males have large antlers for fighting

sensitive nose for smelling danger

males have a growth of skin and hair called a bell

thick, furry coat for keeping warm

a male moose

PLANT EATER

A moose eats only plants. It eats water plants and grass. Moose eat many plants each day.

This female moose is grazing with her young calf.

Morocco

see also: Africa, Desert

Morocco is a country on the northwest coast of Africa. Morocco has mountain ranges and a high, flat area. It has some desert. The coast has hot summers and mild, wet winters.

Living in Morocco

Many people live in the country. Most are farmers. They grow citrus fruit, vegetables, wheat, and barley. Some people work with tourists. Others work in mining and fishing.

Moroccans eat *couscous*. It is made from wheat. The wheat is cracked and then cooked by steaming. Almost anything can be eaten with *couscous*. Stews made of spicy meat and vegetables are favorites.

The covered markets are called bazaars. Whole streets of shops might all sell the same thing. These shops sell things made of brass.

DID YOU KNOW?

Computers are used to help farmers in Morocco. The computers run machines that water the crops.

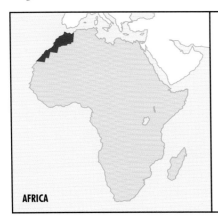

AFRICA

FACT FILE

PEOPLE	Moroccans
POPULATION	about 27 million
MAIN LANGUAGES	Arabic, Berber
CAPITAL CITY	Rabat
MONEY	Dirham
HIGHEST MOUNTAIN	Jebel Toubkal—13,670 feet
LONGEST RIVER	Oued Moulouya—354 miles

Mosquito

see also: Fly, Insects

A mosquito is an insect. It is a small fly. Mosquitoes are found all over the world. They live in warm and wet places. Many mosquitoes carry diseases.

Mosquito families

Mosquitoes do not look after their eggs or babies. A female mosquito lays her eggs in still or slow-flowing water.

MOSQUITO FACTS

NUMBER OF KINDS	3,000
COLOR	brownish
LENGTH	less than one inch
STATUS	common
LIFE SPAN	less than one year
ENEMIES	birds, bats, people

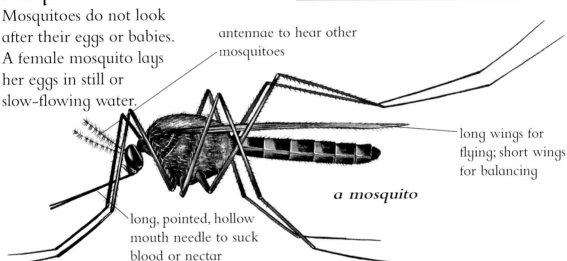

antennae to hear other mosquitoes

long wings for flying; short wings for balancing

a mosquito

long, pointed, hollow mouth needle to suck blood or nectar

A mosquito grows from an egg to an adult mosquito in stages. The eggs hatch into little wormlike larvae. The larvae live in water. A fully-grown larva forms a covering to become a pupa. Then the adult mosquito comes out of the pupa.

PLANT, INSECT, AND MEAT EATER

A mosquito larva eats tiny animals in the water. Adult female mosquitoes drink the blood of humans or animals. Male mosquitoes drink nectar or plant juice.

This mosquito is coming out of its pupa.

Moss

see also: Plants

A moss is a small, green plant. It grows best in damp places. Mosses usually grow close together. They form a mat. They grow all over the world. They do not grow in the sea. They are mostly found on smooth rocks, on trees, and on the ground. Mosses do not have flowers.

The life of moss

A new moss plant grows in two stages. First a male sperm and female egg combine. They grow into a long stalk. The stalk has a capsule at the end. Inside the capsule are thousands of spores. The spores might grow into new moss plants.

Many insects live in mosses. Birds sometimes line their nests with moss. Moss holds water like a sponge. This stops water from draining away. Peat is a spongy kind of soil. It forms from the broken-down remains of peat moss.

Moss grows in cool, dark places. This hair moss has green and red leaves.

MOSS FACTS

NUMBER OF	
KINDS	12 thousand
HEIGHT	up to 6 inches

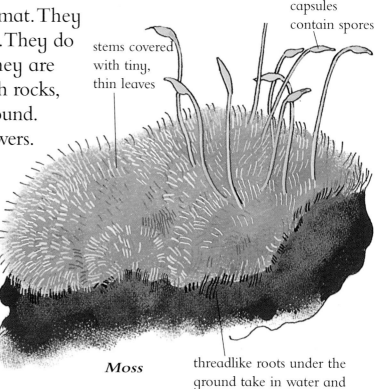

capsules contain spores

stems covered with tiny, thin leaves

Moss

threadlike roots under the ground take in water and hold moss in place

Moth

see also: Butterfly, Caterpillar, Insects, Metamorphosis

A moth is an insect. It has large wings. A moth begins life as a caterpillar. It later changes into a moth. Moths are found all over the world. They fly mostly in the evening or at night.

How moths live

A moth caterpillar eats enough food to become very plump. Then the caterpillar spins a cocoon around itself. It becomes a chrysalis. The caterpillar changes into an a moth inside the chrysalis.

Each kind of moth has a way to avoid enemies. The tiger moth tastes terrible to birds. The buff-tip moth looks like a twig. This helps it hide. The eyed-hawk moth has large eye patterns on its wings. This frightens off enemies.

MOTH FACTS

NUMBER OF	
KINDS	more than 100 thousand
SIZE	less than an inch to 8 inches across
STATUS	some species threatened
LIFE SPAN	up to 3 years
ENEMIES	birds, bats, reptiles, frogs

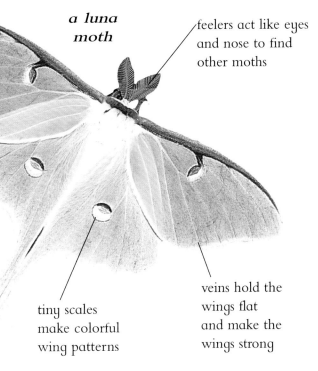

a luna moth

feelers act like eyes and nose to find other moths

veins hold the wings flat and make the wings strong

tiny scales make colorful wing patterns

PLANT EATER

Moths sip sweet juice from flowers and rotting fruit. They eat using a mouth tube. They roll up the mouth tube when they are not drinking.

The caterpillars have hatched from these fox moth eggs.

Motorcycle

see also: Bicycle, Transportation

A motorcycle is a vehicle with two wheels. It carries one or two people. A motorcyle is pushed by the energy from an engine.

The first motorcycles

Motorcycles were invented more than one hundred years ago. The first motorcycles were bicycles with an engine. They were very slow and dangerous. Later more powerful engines were invented. Motorcycles with the new engines could go faster. They could reach speeds of 100 miles per hour. These motorcycles were heavy and hard to steer. Today motorcycles are more comfortable to ride. The frames and engines are lighter. Softer tires absorb the bumps.

Modern motorcycles can travel very fast. They have room for a passenger to sit behind the driver.

This motorcycle and sidecar were the latest thing at a motorshow in 1930. The sidecar had a sliding roof.

How motorcycles are used

All over the world, motorcycles are used for transportation. They do not get stuck in traffic. They use less fuel. They do not cost much to run. Motorcycle riders can get wet and cold in bad weather. Motorcycles are not very safe on icy roads or snow.

MOTORCYCLE FIRSTS

INVENTED	1869
FIRST MADE	1885
FIRST TRACK RACES	1897
FIRST CROSS-COUNTRY RACE	1907

Mountain

see also: Island, Volcano

Mountains are areas of high land. The land has steep, sloping sides. The highest point on a mountain is called the peak. A mountain is usually over 1,600 feet high. Most mountains are part of a large group. The group is called a mountain range or a chain.

How mountains are made

Mountains are usually made when flat layers of rock are pushed by forces in the earth. The layers can be pushed so much that they make giant ripples. The ripples are called *folds.* Some mountains are volcanoes. Molten rock flows out of them. They grow bigger every time they erupt. Some mountains rise from the ocean floor. Their peaks make small islands.

DID YOU KNOW?

The 25 highest mountains in the world are all in the Himalayan and Karakoram mountain ranges. These two ranges are in the same area of Asia. These mountains are still getting bigger.

People and mountains

Not many people live in high mountains. The land can be too steep. The climate can be too cold and wet to grow crops. People can enjoy mountain sports, such as skiing and climbing. Mountains are good places to build reservoirs to store water. Water flows quickly down mountains. It can be used to make electricity in power plants.

Mountains are used for winter sports such as skiing and snowboarding.

Mouse

see also: Mammal

A mouse is a very small mammal. It is about as big as a chicken egg. A mouse is covered in fur. It has a long, thin tail. The word *mice* is used for more than one mouse. Mice have large front teeth for nibbling. They eat nuts and fruit.

Mouse families

A male mouse is called a buck. A female mouse is called a doe. Mouse babies are called cubs. Cubs are born blind, deaf, and hairless. Their eyes open after one week. A doe can give birth to a hundred cubs in one year.

MOUSE FACTS

NUMBER OF	
KINDS	1,082 mice and rats
COLOR	brown, black, white, gray
LENGTH	about 3 inches with a tail the same length
STATUS	common
LIFE SPAN	about 2 years
ENEMIES	cats, birds of prey, people

ears for good hearing

eyes on the sides of the head for all-around vision

claws for gripping

a harvest mouse

tail to balance when running and climbing

PLANT, INSECT, AND MEAT EATER

Wild mice have lived with humans for about 10 thousand years. Houses and farm buildings are warm places to live. There is plenty of food, such as grain. Mice also eat insects and household scraps.

This is a nest of wood mice cubs. They will soon look like their mother.

Music

*see also: Musical Instrument, Jazz,
Classical Music, Percussion Instruments,
String Instruments, Wind Instruments*

Music is making sounds using
voices and instruments. Human
beings have sung and chanted
from earliest times. No one knows
what very early music was like.

Music around the world

There are many different kinds of music.
Each part of the world has its own special
kind of music. Flamenco music
is from Spain. Gamelan music is from
Indonesia. Today many types of music
are made and enjoyed all over the world.
Today's music includes pop music,
classical music, folk, and jazz.

This musician from India is playing
a stringed instrument. It is called a
sitar. India's musical tradition is
hundreds of years old.

*The famous jazz musician Dizzy
Gillespie played his specially-made
trumpet. The trumpet is also played
in popular and classical music.*

Pythagoras (582–500 BC)

The ancient Greek philosopher,
Pythagoras, had some of the earliest ideas
about music. He discovered that
mathematics could be applied to musical
notes. This idea led to the way a lot of
music is composed and written.

Musical Instrument

see also: Music, Percussion Instruments, String Instruments, Wind Instruments

Musical instruments are made for making music. They can be as simple as a triangle. They can also be as complicated as an electronic keyboard. Everyday objects, like spoons or dried seed pods, can also be musical instruments.

Jimi Hendrix (1942–1970)

Jimi Hendrix was an American musician. He played the electric guitar. Hendrix was always looking for new ways to make sounds. In one of his songs, he hummed through a comb covered in paper.

This Aboriginal Australian musician is using a stick to beat out a rhythm.

Jimi Hendrix played the electric guitar. The electric guitar is a very popular modern instrument.

The first instruments

People began by using parts of their bodies to make sounds. They clapped their hands, stamped their feet, and listened to the rhythm of their heartbeats. The first instruments were sticks beating out rhythms.

Instruments today

Today instruments are grouped by the way they make sounds. Some instruments use strings. Some use the musician's breath. Some are hit or shaken. Some make electronic sounds.

Myth

see also: Legend, Literature, Story

Myths are stories about gods, goddesses, and spirits. Myths often try to explain how the world was created. Myths also try to explain how important discoveries, such as fire, were made.

Greek, Roman, and Norse myths

The most famous myths are the myths of the ancient Greeks and Romans, and the Norse myths of the Vikings. These myths tell how the ancient people saw the world. Many myths tell how the gods and goddesses came to Earth and played tricks on or fell in love with human beings.

Myths said that things like thunder and lightning were signs of the gods' anger.

This Native American drum is painted with a mythical bird.

Myths of native people

The Native Americans, the Aborigines in Australia, and the Maoris in New Zealand also have many myths. The myths of different tribes explain how things happened in the world. Most Native American myths are about animals that represent the spirits of the earth.

Native Americans

see also: North America, South America, Bison

Native Americans were the first people of North America. They have lived in North America for about 15-30 thousand years. Today there are about 3 million Native Americans in North America.

DID YOU KNOW?

The name *Indian* was given to Native Americans by the first European explorers. The explorers thought they had reached the area in Asia called the Indies.

Land and life

Native Americans are divided into groups called *tribes*. The Mohawk tribe lived in the northeast. They lived in homes called longhouses. Many families shared the same longhouse. They grew corn and hunted deer.

Tribes such as the Lakota lived on the grassy plains. They lived in teepees. They hunted bison. Their teepees could be taken apart and moved. Then the Lakota could follow the herds of bison.

Some of the Native Americans lived in forests. They used rivers as their roads.

Native Americans today

Most tribes had their land taken from them when European settlers arrived. Many Native Americans were moved to special areas called reservations. Many tribes have kept their traditions alive.

When tribes moved, they carried their belongings on a travois.

Nepal

see also: Asia, Mountain

Nepal is in Asia. It is a small country. It is one of the world's highest countries. Most of Nepal is in the Himalaya Mountains. Almost half of Nepal is covered with forests. It is warmer and wetter lower down in the valleys.

Living in Nepal

Nearly everyone works on farms. Rice and vegetables are the most important crops. Some farmers raise goats, cattle, and buffalo. They also cut down trees to sell the wood. People from the Sherpa tribe often work as mountain guides for tourists and visiting climbers.

Most Nepalese are Hindus. They believe in many gods and goddesses. People often celebrate holy days by washing in a river or lake. They sing and dance to celebrate weddings and farming events.

This cart is part of the Nepalese New Year festival.

DID YOU KNOW?

A Nepalese Sherpa named Tenzing Norgay and the New Zealand mountain climber, Sir Edmund Hillary, were the first people to reach the top of Mount Everest in the Himalayas. They reached the top of the world's tallest mountain on May 29, 1953. They had climbed for two months.

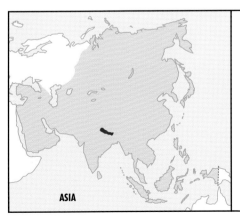

ASIA

FACT FILE

PEOPLE........................Nepalese

POPULATION...............about 21 million

MAIN LANGUAGE.........Nepali

CAPITAL CITY..............Katmandu

MONEY.......................Nepalese rupee

HIGHEST MOUNTAIN... Mount Everest—29,028 feet

LONGEST RIVER...........River Ghaghara—571 miles

Netherlands

see also: Europe

The Netherlands is a country in northwest Europe. It has a coast along the North Sea. Most of the land is low and flat. Some of the land used to be underwater. The people used pumps and walls called *dikes* to drain land. These land areas are called *polders*.

Living in the Netherlands

Dutch farmers grow crops. They raise herds of dairy cows. Dutch cheese is sold in many countries. Some farmers grow tulips and other flowers. There are big factories in the ports of Rotterdam and Amsterdam.

Some of the world's most famous artists were Dutch. The painters Rembrandt, Van Gogh, and Vermeer were born in the Netherlands.

The Netherlands are famous for their tulips and windmills. The windmills used to pump water away from flooded land. Now most pumping is done by big machines.

DID YOU KNOW?

People sometimes call this country Holland. One part of the Netherlands is called Holland, but this is not the correct name for the whole country.

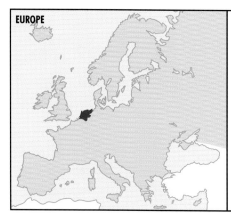

EUROPE

FACT FILE

PEOPLE.................Dutch, Netherlanders

POPULATION.........about 15 million

MAIN LANGUAGE...Dutch

CAPITAL CITY........Amsterdam

MONEY................Euro

HIGHEST LAND......Vaalserberg–1,054 feet

LONGEST RIVER.....River Rhine–820 miles